Original title:
In the Garden of the Tropics

Copyright © 2025 Creative Arts Management OÜ
All rights reserved.

Author: Mariana Leclair
ISBN HARDBACK: 978-1-80581-506-8
ISBN PAPERBACK: 978-1-80581-033-9
ISBN EBOOK: 978-1-80581-506-8

Tropical Tides of Aroma

With mango scents that tease the nose,
I tripped on daisies, oh, how it goes!
A parrot squawks, a monkey grins,
These fruity friends, where chaos begins.

Coconuts roll like bowling balls,
While lizards dance on leafy walls.
The sun's a prankster shining bright,
Tickling palms with its warm light.

Where the Wildflowers Play

Bumblebees buzz in a honeyed race,
While frogs play leapfrog, just for their place.
A cactus winks with a thistle grin,
As ants rehearse a tiny violin.

Sunflowers gossip as the breeze sighs,
They plot to steal the clouds' blue guise.
What mischief blooms in nature's plot,
In this wildflower field, there's always a lot!

The Rhythm of Undulating Vines

Vines twist and twirl like dancers in glee,
While a sloth conducts with a lazy decree.
Every thump and bump adds to the song,
A fruit bat choruses all night long.

The rhythm of leaves rustles in sync,
Where iguanas ponder and pausing to think.
Shadows shimmy beneath the moon's light,
In this vine-clad ballet, everything's bright!

Paradise Found in the Overgrowth

Tangled branches sweep like a broom,
Clearing paths to a leafy room.
Kittens pounce on the vibrant scene,
While butterflies flaunt their kaleidoscope sheen.

The ground is soft with a mossy bed,
Where frogs compete for accolades spread.
Each corner hides a quirky surprise,
As curious critters poke their eyes!

Reflections in a Mountain Stream

Bouncing around like a rubber frog,
I see my face in a lily log.
Fish wink at me with a cheeky grin,
While dragonflies dart, oh where to begin!

The sun's out here, splashing with glee,
As I trip on a root, oh whee, look at me!
Nature's a prankster in this bright scene,
I swear I heard a tree say 'be serene.'

The Eternal Summer's Embrace

The sun's a lazy cat on a warm rock,
While I chase my hat—oh, what a shock!
Coconuts giggle as they drop with a thud,
And my drink's become an awkward mud.

Sandy toes dance with the softest breeze,
While seagulls squawk like they own the seas.
It's a never-ending beach party, I've found,
With trouble as my trusty hound.

Harmony in Color and Breath

Colors collide in playful delight,
Nature's paintbrush throws a wild fight.
A parrot yells at a blush-pink flower,
While laughter blooms like a sunny shower.

Butterflies do the cha-cha and sway,
On a dance floor made of a bright green tray.
Each petal a smile, each leaf's a cheer,
As I giggle through this atmosphere.

Language of the Tropical Breeze

A breeze whispers secrets, cheeky and bold,
Tickling my toes, feeling young not old.
Trees giggle together, swapping their tales,
While the sun draws lines like mischievous trails.

Fruits clash colors, an odd little show,
Bananas play poker with a jolly mango.
I try to join in, but trip on a vine,
And burst out laughing, this moment is fine.

Balmy Nights and Fluttering Secrets

The moon decided to nap on a leaf,
While crickets played tunes, beyond belief.
A frog croaks jokes that make us all cheer,
As fireflies dance, sipping a cold beer.

Lizards gossip like old pals at play,
While shadows tiptoe, stealing the day.
In this wild world, laughter takes flight,
Every creature knows it's a funny night.

The Many-Faceted Rainforest Heart

A parrot wearing glasses reads the news,
With gossip so juicy, it'll give you the blues.
Monkeys steal snacks, they call it their sport,
While sloths take a selfie, with all sorts of snort.

Every crack in the bark hides a prank,
Watch out for frogs, they'll fill up your tank!
With bumbles and fumbles, this jungle's a blast,
In this crazy place, time just moves fast.

Secrets of the Petal Pathways

Butterflies trade secrets, oh what a sight,
They giggle and flutter from morning to night.
Ants march in line like a tiny brigade,
While petals play dress-up, at their jovial parade.

With flowers that snicker and leaves that tease,
There's humor in every sway of the breeze.
Each pathway is lined with emotion and jest,
In this colorful realm, we're always the best.

Glistening Drops on Green Canvas

Dew drops gather like pearls on a string,
A photogenic scene, what joy they bring!
A snail wins the race, in a slow-motion flash,
While telling tall tales in a happy little splash.

With laughter erupting from every tree,
Nature knows how to party with glee.
Under the canopy, silliness reigns,
In this vibrant world, no one has chains.

In Search of the Sunbird's Song

With nectar sweet, they zoom about,
Those tiny birds with joyful spout.
I chased them round, oh what a sight,
Until I tripped, and they took flight.

I asked a parrot for a clue,
He just squawked back, not a word true.
In colors bright, they flit and dance,
While I just hoped for a chance!

The Allure of Ferns and Shadows

Ferns twirl like dancers, quite a show,
But watch your step, don't go too low.
In the shade, they whisper secrets sweet,
While sneaky bugs plot 'round my feet.

The shadows play as light comes through,
Where mischief lurks and laughter grew.
I hear a rustle, a chuckle near,
But it's just a squirrel, never fear!

Journeys Through the Arboreal Maze

A path of leaves, oh which way now?
I lost my map, don't know just how.
But every turn brings joy anew,
As I hear giggles from a distant crew.

Lianas swing like playful ropes,
I'm tangled up, can't find my hopes.
Monkeys laugh high in the trees,
While I look daft, stuck with bees!

Beneath the Fiery Sunset

The sky is painted, orange and red,
A masterpiece above my head.
I raised my gaze, a sight divine,
Until I tripped on an old vine.

As laughter echoed, I took a bow,
The crickets chirped, they know me now.
In twilight's glow, I'll dance along,
And maybe catch a sunbird's song!

Echoes of the Jungle Heart

The monkeys swing, they play their tricks,
While parrots squawk, their feathers mix.
A lizard lounges, with a grin so wide,
As ants march by, in a fearless tide.

The sloth hangs low, in a sleepy daze,
While the toucan's bill draws all the gaze.
A jaguar yawns, on a branch so high,
Not even the loudest shriek could make him fly.

Beneath the Swaying Palms

Coconuts drop with a casual thump,
And nearby, a goat gives a joyful jump.
The breeze is soft, or is it a joke?
As a parrot squawks, a real funny bloke.

A lizard's dance steals the show, oh my!
While crickets chirp, they surely can't fly.
The sun dips low, colors start to blend,
As laughter echoes, and we just pretend.

Nectar's Sweet Embrace

Hummingbirds hover, with a buzz and a spin,
While bees form a line, they're ready to win.
The flowers chuckle, with petals so bright,
As nectar's allure makes the whole scene light.

In this sweet realm, all creatures conspire,
To sip on the drinks that spark such desire.
A bumblebee trips on a petal so grand,
As the butterflies laugh, it's all quite planned.

Mirage of Tropical Twilight

As twilight falls, the frogs start to croak,
While fireflies twinkle, with a giggly poke.
A shadowy figure, oh what a fright,
Turns out to be just the moon's silly light.

The night blooms lovely, with scents so sweet,
As crickets chirp out a dancing beat.
With every giggle, the stars wink back,
In this funny realm where the joy's never lack.

Harmony in the Tropical Wilderness

Frogs in tuxedos leap with flair,
Dancing with lizards, what a pair!
Monkeys trade jokes and swing so free,
While parrots squawk, "Look at me!"

Coconuts bob like heads in the breeze,
Palm trees whisper, "Take it with ease!"
Bees buzz loudly, they think they're cool,
While ants march by like a tiny school.

Sunsets paint the sky like a show,
While iguanas bask, putting on a slow glow.
This festive life, a circus so grand,
In nature's heart, where joys are planned.

The night brings stars that twinkle and tease,
While fireflies dance, aiming to please.
Everyone's giggling, sharing delight,
Under the moon, laughter takes flight!

The Tapestry of Verdant Growth

Vines like ribbons twist and twirl,
While chubby sloths give a lazy whirl.
Bumblebees wear little hats too,
Pollinating flowers, oh what a view!

Turtles take selfies by the stream,
Fish flash smiles, living the dream.
Frogs jump high with sneaky glee,
Claiming the title of king or queen bee!

Papayas drop just to make a splash,
And monkeys giggle, causing a clash.
Each petal waving like a good friend,
This tapestry of life, it has no end.

When the sun dips low, colors ignite,
Fireflies blink, 'It's party time tonight!'
With every flutter, a tale unfolds,
Of laughter and joy that never gets old.

Under the Gaze of the Banyan Tree

The banyan watches with ancient eyes,
As turtles trade tales of the skies.
Caterpillars plan their next big leap,
While the breeze carries secrets we keep.

Squirrels wear capes, soaring with cheer,
Chasing each other without a fear.
The old tree chuckles, swaying so wide,
While critters gather for a fun ride.

Crickets play music, a symphony sweet,
As night brings a dance, oh what a treat!
Fireflies twinkle like stars in disguise,
Under the gaze where laughter never dies.

With every rustle, a parting joke,
The banyan tree smiles, gently it spoke.
"Let's share some stories of the day,
In this vibrant playground, come out and play!"

Shadows of Lushness and Light

In shadows where laughter likes to sneak,
Lizards gossip, and frogs peek.
Bananas whisper in playful tones,
"Who stole my peel? It's broken bones!"

Gum trees giggle, releasing their gum,
While puffy clouds look out, feeling numb.
Dancing leaves in a gentle breeze,
Mocking the branches with flapping tease.

Jungles filled with chatter and cheer,
Every heartbeat, a joke you can hear.
Crabs doing limbo, all in a line,
While sunlight sprinkles, oh so fine.

As day slips away, colors ignite,
The wildlife laughs under soft moonlight.
With mischief galore, beneath starry night,
"Tell me your secrets, let's hold them tight!"

Shadows Lengthen in Paradise

Sunshine plays tag with the clouds,
Lizards dance on sun-kissed shrouds.
Coconuts tumble, rolling away,
Who needs a drink? Just pop and play.

Monkeys swing through the grapevine,
Stealing fruits, thinking they're divine.
A parrot squawks, tries to outsing,
While a frog croaks, 'What a fling!'

Tropical fish paint the ocean bright,
They gossip of turtles taking flight.
As shadows stretch, the laughter sounds,
In this paradise, joy abounds.

The Language of Tropical Breezes

Winds whisper secrets through the trees,
Tickling leaves, with teasing ease.
A breeze giggles, 'Let's go play,'
While flowers blush through the day.

Swaying palms wave back with glee,
Each frond a friend, come dance with me.
The sun winks with a golden glow,
As colors clash in a vibrant show.

Butterflies chat in colors bold,
Trading stories, both new and old.
'Who knew a gust could tickle so?'
In these whispers, joy starts to grow.

Beneath the Canopy's Gentle Veil

Beneath the leaves, the shadows tease,
A carpet of herbs and buzzing bees.
The sloth takes a nap, quite profound,
While ants march like a circus round.

Laughter erupts from a hidden vine,
As chameleons change, looking fine.
'Who do you think you're fooling today?'
Says a cheeky bird, just on display.

The canopy hides such strange delights,
With critters playing their quirky fights.
In this lush haven, each creature's prime,
In humor's embrace, we pass the time.

Roots That Reach for the Sky

Roots wiggle beneath the sunlit ground,
Hoping for mischief yet to be found.
They dream of dancing on soft blue air,
But instead, they're stuck down there.

Big leaves flap as if having fun,
Playing hide and seek with the sun.
'Come join the party,' the ferns declare,
'We're the coolest plants with flair to spare!'

Cacti joke about being pointy,
While vines decide to go all groovy.
In this jungle, laughter thrives,
Where every critter joyfully jives.

Celestial Drifts Above Canopy

Above the green, the clouds do dance,
A squirrel struts in his dapper pants.
He spins and twirls like he's the king,
While birds all laugh at his silly fling.

Beneath the shade where shadows play,
A turtle gabs about his day.
He's slow and steady, with tales so thick,
Of a race he lost to a hopping stick.

The flowers giggle, their petals bright,
As bees do buzz with sheer delight.
They've heard the jokes, they've spread them wide,
It's a flower party, come join the ride!

So underneath this lively space,
Every critter sprints with grace.
In this realm where laughter looms,
Nature's fun spills from the blooms.

A Tapestry of Wild Encounters

A parrot squawks in colors bold,
His tales of treasure, oh so told.
With feathers bright, he jokes with flair,
While monkeys swing through fragrant air.

A sloth hangs low, he strikes a pose,
Looking chill in his leafy clothes.
He yawns wide, "What's the rush today?
I'll get to it…maybe next May."

The iguanas wear their frowny face,
Grumpy puppets in a lazy race.
Their slow-paced stroll, a sight to see,
While chattering frogs compete with glee.

As laughter echoes through this show,
Nature's quirks do steal the glow.
The tapestry bright, wild joy displayed,
A hum of chaos, a grand parade.

Habitat of the Untamed Spirit

A raccoon dons his nighttime mask,
Sneaking snacks is his favorite task.
With pies and sweets, he eyes the plate,
But trips on roots—oh, his silly fate!

A hedgehog plots his grand escape,
From thorny hugs, he'll reshape.
"Why, oh why, do they love to squeeze?
I'm not a toy, I'm just here to tease!"

The fireflies flash their disco light,
Dancing between the ferns at night.
They giggle loud, "Hey, catch this glow!"
Racing round in a rhythmic flow.

This habitat, wild and free,
Is filled with laughter, can't you see?
Amongst the fun and silly cheer,
The spirit thrives from far and near.

Celestial Drip of Morning Dew

Beneath the sun's giggle, dew drops play,
A slippery dance, they cling and sway.
A bee buzzes loudly, dons a tiny hat,
Sipping nectar like it's a tea party chat.

Lizards lounge lazily, on leaves they stick,
Hiding from rain, oh, the weather's a trick!
They gossip of clouds like it's the best news,
While ants march around in their tiny shoes.

Joyful blooms open, a party began,
Each flower a dancer, as bright as they can.
With colors that wink and lightly tease,
They giggle at gnomes planting oddities with ease.

The world is a circus, with critters in show,
Performing their antics, from fast to slow.
When twilight arrives, they'll rest — oh, what fun,
In the morning, they'll rise, for another round run.

Brushstrokes of Color in Hidden Glades

A paintbrush of laughter, the skies have a flair,
Splashes of flora, beyond compare.
Marigolds frolic, while daisies jive,
Swaying to tunes as bees take a dive.

Caterpillars chatter, wearing bright stripes,
They're style icons, with their curious gripes.
Leaves wave their hands, it's a leafy salute,
As squirrels debate if they'll wear their new suit.

Sunlight dribbles like melted gold,
Tickling the shadows, brave and bold.
While frogs jump high, hoping for cheers,
They croak silly songs that tickle your ears.

In corners where giggles twirl and spin,
Nature's an artist, bringing laughter within.
With the canvas alive, each petal a muse,
A riot of colors, let's sip morning's brew.

Amidst the Verdant Thicket

Critters convene, holding a hearty feast,
Chomp and chatter, nature's lively beast.
A hedgehog plays chess, with snails for the crew,
While rabbits bet carrots, who'll win it anew?

Tiny trees gossip about the day's plans,
They canopy secrets, with fluttering hands.
Birds paint their songs, a melodious spree,
Each note a high-five from tree to tree.

The groundhog peeks out, with a cheeky grin,
Declares it's a party, let the fun begin!
Bushes are giggling at the tickling breeze,
As ladybugs flutter, aiming to please.

Oh, what a humor in this tangled abode,
Where even the roots hold a comedic code.
The nature parade leads to laughs and cheers,
In the whimsical jungles, forget all your fears.

Dappled Light and Chasing Shadows

The sun throws confetti, it's a wild affair,
Shadows dance sideways, without a care.
Moths don disguises, in the fading light,
While crickets hold concerts, their voices polite.

The grass tickles toes, as the children run,
Squeals drift from flowers, a giggly pun.
A squirrel vaults high, tries to steal the show,
With acorn acrobatics, for all in tow.

As twilight approaches, the fireflies glow,
They're lanterns of mischief, setting the flow.
Beneath the tall palms, the laughter grows loud,
In this carnival of leaves, the critters are proud.

With mischief and nonsense, the night takes flight,
In dappled light's wink, every heart feels light.
So join in the revels, where joy spills anew,
In the realm of the silly and antics askew.

A Haven of the Iridescent Beings

The beetles wear their shiny suits,
Dancing like it's prom for brutes.
They twirl beneath the swaying trees,
While crickets hum their silly tease.

The parrots squawk with gossip loud,
As if they're top of their proud crowd.
They sip from nectar like it's wine,
And toast to sunshine, oh so fine!

The frogs are crooning in their croaks,
Confessing love in silly jokes.
A chorus from the pond so bright,
In harmony, they own the night.

With fireflies flickering like stars,
Counting critters in their cars.
This vibrant place of playful schemes,
Is where laughter sprouts like dreams.

Olfactory Journeys Through the Green

The flowers bloom with scents divine,
Old nettles sneer, 'You call this fine?'
While honeysuckles sway and sway,
Stealing hearts in a perfume play.

The citrus fruits are smiling bright,
With tangy jokes that spark delight.
But mangoes with their sticky gleam,
Beware, they may just steal your dream!

Coconut falls, bonk on the head,
Leaving one mad with thoughts of bread.
The scent of rain like laughter's song,
Is where all silly things belong.

As laughter wafts on warming breeze,
The scents engage in antics, tease.
With noses twitching, all around,
The playful aroma knows no bounds!

Tangles of Roots and Rebirth

The roots are tangled, what a sight,
Dancing legs of nature's fight.
Vines whisper secrets, giggle loud,
'Get tangled up, join our crowd!'

The seedlings sprout with nervous laughs,
As ants parade in silly halves.
They march in lines, a comical show,
Grab snacks for their long journey, whoa!

An old trunk chuckles, wise and stout,
Telling tales of what's about.
'Gravity's joke, I can't believe,
How high can you climb? Just don't leave!'

This quirky maze, a work of art,
Where every twist is nature's heart.
Amidst the roots, they twist and sway,
Rebirth in laughter, every day!

The Voice of the Tropical Night

The night spills over with froggy croons,
As fireflies zap like little loons.
Owls hoot jokes from branch to branch,
While monkeys plan their mid-night dance.

With every rustle, whispers swell,
The posh raccoon's not one to tell.
His mask of mischief beams a grin,
'Who stole the fruit? Let the fun begin!'

The wind joins in, a breeze of glee,
'Tell me your secrets under the tree!'
With giggles echoing on the air,
The night's alive, a joyous affair.

So listen close, and you might hear,
The laughter spilling, bright and clear.
In this tropical symphony,
Every sound's a burst of glee!

The Color of Eden's Breath

Green frogs wearing top hats,
Prance about on lily pads.
Their jokes, a croak and splat,
Leave the crickets feeling bad.

A parrot with a booming tongue,
Mocks the toucan's fancy beak.
Giggling leaves all around,
It's a comic scene so unique.

Tropical fish in a bowl,
Dance like they're at a ball.
Wiggle, wiggle, no control,
In their colorful overhauls.

Lizards lounge on a bright day,
Sunbathing with goofy grins.
They hear the toucans play,
And join in with silly spins.

Fluttering Wings and Earthy Hues

Butterflies in polka dots,
Fancy dresses in the sun.
Chasing breezes, tangled knots,
Who knew flowers had such fun?

Moths at night in disco lights,
Twirl beneath the silver moon.
Mimicking the stars in flights,
Dancing to a nature tune.

Beetles wear their shiny shells,
Like rollerblades on garden lanes.
With a laugh, the ladybug yells,
Rolling on her little trains.

Sunset glow in funny shades,
Shapes of animals come alive.
All-night party serenades,
Where the wild things thrive and jive.

Serenade of Rainforest Blooms

Petals sharing all the gossip,
Whispering secrets on the vine.
They giggle, hiding from a slip,
As raindrops fall, oh how divine!

Bumblebees wear tiny hats,
Buzzing tunes in blooming flair.
Their sweet dance with fancy spins,
Make the flowers stop and stare.

Colorful frogs write ballads,
With nighttime tunes under the tree.
They croak a tune, slowly add,
Funny verses—who will it be?

Glittering bugs in a slow shimmy,
Throwing parties in a swirl.
The night air has a joyful whimsy,
Nature's laughter makes hearts twirl.

Sunlight Kissing Orchid Faces

Orchids smile with sunny cheer,
Pouting petals when it rains.
Adding jokes to every sphere,
Mimicking the sunlight's gains.

Bees don sunglasses for the day,
Sipping nectar like a drink.
Buzzing truths in their own way,
Playful chats as they all think.

Vines and creepers twine so tight,
Turning silly shapes and styles.
Twirling around with delight,
Engines of nature's crazy wiles.

A flutter of wings draws a crowd,
As butterflies play hide and seek.
Joyful laughter, warm and loud,
Nature's comedy at its peak.

The Poetry of Endangered Blooms

In a leafy dress, the blooms do sway,
They dance with bees, who've lost their way.
A parrot shouts, 'What's that you say?'
'Watch out for cats, they'll ruin our play!'

Nectar drips like candy from above,
But here comes a slug, all slimy with love.
He slips and slides, thinks he's a dove,
While ants hold a party, push come to shove!

Under sunlit beams, all wildlife prance,
The squirrel stole my salad, what a chance!
Laughter erupts, what a comical dance,
In this wild world, all get a glance.

So raise a toast with a leaf in the air,
For blooms at risk, let's show our care.
May humor thrive, spread joy everywhere,
For in this chaos, who needs despair?

Lullaby of the Shimmering Petal

Twinkle, twinkle, little leaf,
A bug takes rest, beyond belief.
'Please don't snore!' cries a tiny thief,
As ladybugs giggle, full of mischief.

The flower hums a sleepy tune,
While frogs croak softly, under the moon.
Fireflies flicker, a dazzling boon,
'You've got some flair, you little cartoon!'

In this wild choir, all join in song,
A raucous harmony, that can't be wrong.
While sloths hang out,so lazy and strong,
Just another night, where all belong.

So dream of petals, so shiny and bright,
With creatures galore, a wacky sight.
In this tropical realm, feel the delight,
As slumber hugs us, soft as the night.

Whispers of the Rainforest

Listen close, the trees tell tales,
Of wiggly worms and colorful snails.
A monkey swings, wearing hand-me-downs,
'Why wear a suit when I can wear frowns?'

Caterpillars gossip, dressed up in stripes,
While chattering parrots share wild gripes.
A toucan jokes, saying 'Who needs pipes?'
When he's got a beak that's full of hype!

Underneath the ferns, a dance does start,
With jitterbugs grooving, oh so smart.
They flash their colors, a comical art,
With beetles and butterflies picking apart.

So join the chatter, the fun won't cease,
In this lush world, let humor increase.
For every leaf holds stories of peace,
While laughter blossoms, our joy won't decrease.

Lush Canopies and Hidden Dreams

Above the jungle, dreams take flight,
Where vines entwine and stars shine bright.
A sloth yawned, 'It's too much height,'
'Just me and my snack, what a lovely sight!'

The capybara lounges, wears shades so cool,
Sipping on nectar, it's his favorite fuel.
While toucans strut, breaking every rule,
Their flashy outfits, nature's own school!

As shadows dance on the forest floor,
A wild boar snorts, 'What's behind that door?'
With laughter echoing, we all explore,
In this tropical world, there's so much to adore!

So here's to the greens, and all that gleams,
In every corner, reality seems,
A place for laughter, big dreams and schemes,
In a quirky kingdom, where fun redeems.

The Breath of Fragrant Nights

Beneath the stars and laughing moons,
The flowers gossip about their prunes.
A monkey swings with flair and style,
While ants march on, all in a pile.

A parrot squawks a silly song,
The night air feels so right, not wrong.
Lizards dance on branches high,
While fireflies wink and blink, oh my!

Coconuts drop with a thump and roll,
The night's adventure takes its toll.
A cat takes aim with wide-eyed grin,
But misses the fun and joins the din.

In this wild place where laughter flows,
Each petal's whisper, a joke that glows.
Tropical nights, a whimsical show,
Where the silly animals steal the show.

Serpents in the Sunlit Shade

A snake slides by with a sassy sway,
He stops to chat, not much to say.
His belly's full of mangoes bright,
He burps so loud it brings delight!

Lizards sunbathe, striking poses cool,
One falls asleep, he's such a fool.
A squirrel mocks with a tiny cheer,
"Don't snooze too long, or disappear!"

The sun plays tricks, it's hard to tell,
Which tree's a friend and which one's a shell.
A branch breaks under a heavy weight,
And down drops a bird—it's quite the fate!

All creatures laugh in the dappled light,
Serpents slither in fancy flight.
With every flicker, a silly ruse,
In sunlit shade, there's joy to choose.

Mystique of the Canopy Floor

The forest floor is a tangled mess,
Where a beetle lost his fancy dress.
He struts around with prideful glee,
   Underneath a leaf, sipping tea.

A dancing tree frog leaps and bounds,
While whispers echo all around.
"Did you hear the snail's big plan?"
"A race to the brambles, who can, who can?"

Nutty squirrels steal the show, so sly,
They hide their stash and laugh and cry.
A flower sneezes, "Excuse me, please!"
And tickles the breeze with effortless ease.

Creatures giggle through the vibrant maze,
In this strange place, they're all in a daze.
Each turn reveals a funny surprise,
A world of quirks beneath the skies.

Crickets' Serenade at Twilight

As twilight falls, the crickets sing,
Their chorus loud, a joyful fling.
A firefly winks, "Join in the fun!"
While shadows play till the day is done.

A hedgehog rolls in a ball so round,
He tumbles down without a sound.
The cricket band begins to sway,
With all the beats they can convey.

The moon peeks out, a silly face,
It grins and glows with charm and grace.
A frog hops in, a scuffle ensues,
"Hey buddy, share those dancing shoes!"

In the glow of night, there's laughter bright,
As every critter finds delight.
With jokes and jigs and giddy dreams,
They celebrate with silly schemes.

The Symphony of Leafy Giants

When the trees start to dance, oh what a sight,
The leaves play a tune, from morning till night.
A parrot chuckles, with a vibrant flair,
While a sloth makes a solo, hanging mid-air.

A mischievous monkey swings with great glee,
Tickling the branches, as happy as can be.
From gentle breezes to rustling sounds,
The leafy giants make fun all around.

Their roots tap to rhythms, a beat on the ground,
Creating a concert in nature profound.
The sun beams down, with a twinkling eye,
Laughing at squirrels who leap and fly high.

When night falls down, the crickets take part,
Joining the chorus; it's a musical art.
In this leafy kingdom, the fun never ends,
Nature's own laughter, forever transcends.

Shadows and Sunbeams Intertwined

Sunbeams peek through, like a playful tease,
Dancing with shadows, swaying in the breeze.
A lizard attempts a ballet on a stone,
While a weary old turtle complains with a groan.

The flowers all giggle, bright colors exposed,
As bees in their suits buzz around, so composed.
Each petal's a face, with comedic grins,
Sharing the humor as the day begins.

A butterfly flutters, trying to be sly,
But trips on a leaf and gives a loud cry.
The grasshoppers laugh, doing cheeky little hops,
As sunbathing turtles pass out with their flops.

The shadows stretch longer, the fun's far from done,
As the day's chaotic dance winds up with the sun.
In this playful realm, where laughter aligns,
Every corner whispers, "Oh, what silly times!"

Fluttering Wings in Glistening Light

With a flap and a flutter, here comes a bright show,
A carnival of colors, putting on a glow.
Cockatoos hoot, all decked in their best,
While dragonflies zoom in a fanciful quest.

The butterflies giggle, in twirls they delight,
Chasing each other in a dazzling flight.
A toucan chimes in with a honk and a laugh,
As birds form a band, each sound their own staff.

A hummingbird zooms, with energy, so spry,
Spinning in circles 'neath the wide-open sky.
While geckos grumble from high up a tree,
Their comments hilariously stuck in the leaf spree.

The light starts to dim, but joy doesn't fade,
As the stars appear bright on this playful parade.
Each fluttering wing, a burst of pure cheer,
In this whimsical world, only laughter is near.

Jewel Tones of a Hidden World

In a realm of treasures, colors take flight,
Emeralds and sapphires twinkle so bright.
A crab in its shell tries to win a race,
While a slow-moving snail grins with silly grace.

The flowers wear jewels, sparkling in dew,
As ants march in line, making plans for a stew.
Each petal, a canvas, adorned with delight,
In shades of the rainbow, oh what a sight!

A chameleon chuckles, changing its hue,
Imitating friends, it's a colorful crew.
"Catch me if you can!" cries a bright little bee,
While the toadstools all giggle, hidden near the tree.

The dance of the critters, a laugh in the night,
As the moon keeps on shining, casting its light.
In a jewel-toned world, where the fun spins around,
The laughter of nature is joyfully found.

Secrets Beneath the Palms

Beneath the palms, a coconut fell,
A squirrel donned it, looked like a bell.
He ran with flair, as if in a race,
Chasing a breeze with a nutty face.

Lizards sunbathe, trying to tan,
While frogs discuss their latest plan.
They croak and hop, a comedic scene,
Debating who's the marble machine!

A parrot squawks, "Let's throw a dance!"
With a wiggle and jiggle, he took a chance.
His friends all joined, a tropical show,
Who knew birds liked a good limbo low?

The breeze brings secrets, whispers of fun,
Where everything sparkles under the sun.
Silly sounds fill this vibrant place,
Life's a circus, with laughter as grace.

Sun-Kissed Petals of Paradise

Flowers gossip in colors so bright,
They prance and twirl in morning light.
One petal whispers, "I'm the best-dressed!"
While another sighs, "I'm just stressed!"

A bee buzzes in, quite the amateur spy,
"Life's not a race, just enjoy the pie!"
Dancing on daisies, a butterfly sighed,
"Are we all just winging it? Take it in stride!"

The breeze tickles skin like a mischievous friend,
A playful breeze making flowers bend.
They giggle and jive, all in a twist,
In this sunny place, how could you resist?

So here's to petals, vibrant and free,
Spreading their laughter—come join the spree!
With fruit punch laughter and sunshine so sweet,
Life's just a party, let's all take a seat.

Echoes of Tropical Bliss

A monkey swings with a flair so grand,
Dressed in a hat, he's got a band!
Chasing a dream, he strums a tune,
While birds join in, from morn till noon.

The flowers dance to a beat so sly,
They bounce and sway, oh me, oh my!
One flower giggles, "I have the best scent!"
While another rolls her eyes, "I pay my rent!"

The sun sets low, like a tired face,
Blushing the sky, oh, what a place!
Crickets start singing, it's their big night,
While fireflies twinkle, a glowing delight.

As shadows lengthen and laughter flows,
A chorus of joy in the evening glows.
Life's a sweet echo, a whimsical thrill,
In this playful paradise, we dance at will.

Vibrant Hues of Nature's Canvas

Colors splash like paint from a can,
Nature shows off, a wild art plan.
A pink flamingo strikes a pose so bold,
While giggly flowers share stories untold.

The breeze steals kisses from banana leaves,
Making them whisper and tease like thieves.
A gecko giggles, "I can stick like glue!"
To every sweet moment, he'll stick with you.

The sunset giggles, splashing orange and red,
While sleepy clouds fluff up their bed.
The moon peeks out, a cheeky grin,
"Let's start the night, let the fun begin!"

Laughter echoes under starlit laughs,
Where everything dances in playful crafts.
So come, let's celebrate, with vigor and cheer,
In this vibrant land, joy is always near.

Mandolin Melodies Under Tropical Stars

Under starlit skies, we pluck our strings,
Laughter dances, and the nightbird sings.
A monkey joins with claps so grand,
Twirling on a branch, a true rock band.

Coconuts roll, we dodge with glee,
A rhythm game with a coconut spree.
Banjos, ukuleles, oh what a fright,
The iguana's our judge tonight!

A Mosaic of Colorful Life

Birds in bright coats do the cha-cha slide,
While lizards on branches take great pride.
A toucan's beak, a painter's delight,
Splashing colors from morning to night.

Butterflies flirt and sip from blooms,
Bees waltz around in the buzzing rooms.
Who knew a garden could host such a show?
A carnival of critters with nowhere to go!

The Cascade of Morning Dew

In the dawn's glow, the droplets gleam,
Gliding down leaves, they form a stream.
Frogs in tuxedos greet the new day,
While snails with top hats take the mainway.

Ticklish toes in the fresh cool grass,
Wiggly worms join the morning mass.
With giggles and splashes, the morning breaks,
A party of critters for everyone's shakes!

Beneath the Hibiscus Blooms

Under blossoms, a feast of delight,
Squirrels throw acorns in playful flight.
A gecko in shades, oh what a sight,
Dancing the hula under the moonlight!

Fruits fall down, a soft thud on ground,
As bees buzz around, like notes that abound.
With every snicker from vines all around,
Nature's a joker, in silence profound!

Vibrations of the Tropical Breeze

A parrot laughs, a monkey sways,
The swing of leaves in dance displays.
A breeze brings whispers of cheeky tales,
As lizards strut, wearing tiny pales.

Sun beats down with a golden grin,
While squirrels race in a furry spin.
The flowers giggle, colorful and bright,
As bees buzz by, a comical flight.

Frogs croak tunes, out of sync with each,
While turtles crawl slow, just beyond reach.
The rhythm of life, a carnival spree,
In this wild realm, so carefree, you'll see.

With every flutter and flapping wing,
Nature plays tricks, oh what joy it brings!
A jungle jukebox of funny sounds,
In this vibrant world, laughter abounds.

The Secret Life of Vines

Vines twist and twirl, a playful dance,
They weave their tales, given half a chance.
A chameleon joins, with colors to show,
While sloths hang back, taking it slow.

In shadows they whisper, secrets unfold,
As squirrels play tag, so daring, so bold.
A snake glides past, gives a wink and a nod,
While flowers gossip, all a bit odd.

They tie up the fence, a vine-bound prank,
To a curious frog, they offer a flank.
With sunlight beckoning, laughter ignites,
The garden erupts into comical sights.

From tangled embrace, a scene so absurd,
Nature's own funny, a twist, an unheard.
In this leafy labyrinth, joy intertwines,
Breathing humor, these spirited vines.

Echoes of the Coconut Grove

Coconuts drop, thud on the ground,
With a cheeky grin, they roll around.
Palm trees sway, sharing secrets in breeze,
While crabs wear crowns, with utmost ease.

A parrot squawks, demanding a treat,
While iguanas munch on a snack so sweet.
With each little laugh, a giggle resounds,
In this playful grove, joy knows no bounds.

Beneath the boughs, shadows play tricks,
As little ants march, minds full of tricks.
They form a parade, a comical show,
Nature's jesters, stealing the glow.

With the sun dipping low, a show must unfold,
The rhythm of laughter, a sight to behold.
In the grove of coconuts, life jests and sings,
A playful escape where humor takes wing.

Guardians of the Emerald Realm

Beneath the leaves, a turtle prances,
With snappy jokes, it often glances.
A raccoon snickers, tales quite absurd,
As shadows race past, not a whisper heard.

Each tree stands tall, a jester in green,
Guardians of laughter, a whimsical scene.
With snickerdoodle vines and chuckles galore,
Nature's own humor we can't ignore.

Squirrels hold council, all clad in fur,
Plotting a prank, with just a tiny stir.
A firefly winks, a glowing bard,
Crafting a play, how utterly hard!

With every rustle and fluttering wing,
The emerald guards know all the right things.
In this kingdom of fun, life's never so still,
Where laughter and joy reign, it's pure thrill.

The Allure of Whispering Leaves

The leaves chatter softly, oh what a scene,
They gossip like neighbors, so sardonic and keen.
A parrot near mocks, with a squawk and a flair,
While a turtle names recipes, if folks cease to stare.

In a dance of the ferns, spiders twirl with delight,
One thinks he's a ballerina, oh what a sight!
The flowers, they chuckle, with colors so bright,
As beetles debate who has the best bite.

Butterflies flit by, with secrets to keep,
One worries his date will fall fast asleep.
While cockatoos laugh, and play with their hair,
"Who knew being green could be such a dare?"

A breeze sways the branches, tickling the air,
While crickets compose hits though nobody cares.
In this funny assembly, under sunlight and shade,
Life's quirks are on display, and nobody's afraid.

Palette of Dazzling Tropics

A canvas of colors splashes the ground,
With hues that are spinning, all whirling around.
The sunflowers gossip in yellow delight,
"Who wore it better, the vine or the night?"

The ants wear their stripes like a fashion parade,
While lizards strike poses, "Look how I've displayed!"
A flamboyant bird swoops in with a grin,
"Dare you to try and keep up with my spin!"

Bamboo clinks glasses under the sway,
"Cheers to the bugs who've come out to play!"
In this circus of life where joy's in the air,
Even the old oak chuckles without a care.

Rain splashes paint, as puddles join in,
While frogs try to croak out the latest pop spin.
In this riot of colors, bright laughter is king,
Who knew gardening could lead to such bling?

A Chorus of Exotic Notes

The evening sky hums with a jazzy delight,
While crickets compose tunes in the fading light.
A frog on the lily breaks into a rap,
As owls do the backup, setting quite the trap.

Beneath the bright moon, the tropics unite,
With dance-steps of breezes, twirls of pure light.
A chorus of creatures, all geared up to sing,
While a toucan brings style, like it's his own fling.

The coconuts giggle as palm trees sway wide,
Each rhythm a laugh, with no reason to hide.
While kids on a swing shout out in glee,
"Nature's a concert, just check out the spree!"

So gather your friends, leave your worries behind,
In this orchestra, let joy be defined.
With beats and with laughter, let's dance till we're sore,
The night is our stage; what else could we ask for?

The Promise Beneath the Palms

Underneath the green, there's a whispering cheer,
As critters exchange tales that only they hear.
Swaying palms gossip about the latest gossip,
With a coconut nod, life's tumbles and flop.

The sun tickles cheeks, while shadows make plays,
As monkeys compete in their own funny ways.
One slips on a banana, lands flat on his back,
While others all chuckle, "What a real whack!"

A gecko in shades struts with such grand flair,
In his mind, he's a superstar beyond all compare.
While scents of the fruits tease the senses so sweet,
"Who needs a banquet? Just bring us a treat!"

So come and enjoy, where the laughter runs deep,
With flowers and creatures, their secrets in heap.
In the shade of the palms, there's enchantment galore,
In a land full of wonders, who could ask for more?

Dance of the Exotic Blooms

Butterflies strutted in their bright attire,
Dancing like they've caught some wild desire.
Hummingbirds buzzed, sipping nectar with glee,
While flowers giggled, 'What a sight to see!'

Lizards play poker by the garden's path,
Counting their chips in a game of math.
Monkeys swing in, throwing jokes with a swing,
Saying, 'Who knew plants could do such a thing!'

A parrot proclaimed, 'Let's all laugh and cheer!'
While ants marched in, hosting their own beer.
They toasted to blooms, not forgetting the sun,
In this tropical wonder, where life is pure fun!

As night gently falls with a moonlit swoon,
The stars start to twinkle, oh, what a cartoon!
The frogs serenade with their ribbiting tune,
And the whole garden laughs beneath the full moon!

Beneath the Banyan's Embrace

Under the banyan, where shadows recline,
Twirling around in a circle so fine.
Squirrels with top hats lead a nut-baking show,
While crickets conduct an orchestra, too!

A group of old turtles sings off-key with flair,
Chasing their tails, without a single care.
The roots whisper secrets of grasshopper pranks,
While the breeze joins in, giving laughs to the banks.

Fireflies flash like they're at a disco rave,
While lizards breakdance, so cool and so brave.
'Why not join in?', shouts the wise old crow,
And all of them giggle as the party starts to grow!

Soon, the moon shines down, with a wink oh so bright,
Creating a backdrop for their wild delight.
Beneath the banyan, they dance with such style,
Nature's own revelers, making life worthwhile!

Castles of Green and Gold

In mighty castles of green and of gold,
Lived crickets and beetles, both clever and bold.
The king was a frog with a crown made of leaves,
He ruled over brambles, and all who believes!

The queen was a spider, spinning webs of lace,
Hosting grand banquets, a grand bug ballet space.
The ants served the snacks, wearing tiny chef hats,
While butterfly waiters flitted with spats.

They danced the cha-cha on grass-blade towers,
And rain poured confetti of colorful flowers.
'This feast is divine!' yelled a giddy old bee,
Who buzzed and twirled, as happy as can be!

As dusk turned to night, they twinkled in bliss,
With stars as their chandeliers, nothing amiss.
In castles of green, their laughter took flight,
A home full of joy, spinning magic at night!

Enchanted Oasis of Serenity

An oasis of giggles, with palms high and proud,
Where whispers of mischief echo quite loud.
Frogs hop on lily pads, leaping with cheer,
While turtles float by, just sipping some beer.

The waiter, a crab, with a tray full of sand,
Serves cocktails of seaweed, it's all quite grand.
Funny fish flip-flop, trying to catch a breeze,
While a wise old owl points, saying, "Do as you please!"

A parade of bright shells starts strutting their stuff,
With sea urchins bopping, now that's just enough!
They twirl in the waves, with dolphins in sync,
Saying, 'Join in our fun, don't you dare just think!'

As the sun starts to set, painting skies oh so bold,
The laughter grows stronger, a sight to behold.
In this oasis where joy is the key,
Funny creatures unite, so wild and so free!

Petals and Dreams in Midnight Blue

Underneath the moonlit glow,
Dancing petals steal the show,
A monkey swings, a parrot squawks,
While frogs do their silly talks.

Dreams of flowers twist and twirl,
In the night, the colors swirl,
A breeze teases, a lizard grins,
As nature's party truly begins.

Jasmine giggles, roses sway,
A chameleon begins to play,
While crickets tune a lively beat,
In this place, no one feels beat.

So come along, embrace the fun,
Chase the stars until we've spun,
In midnight hues, let's take a chance,
Join the Verde tropical dance!

The Dance of the Lush Undergrowth

In the thickets, life does run,
Thick vines twist, and ferns have fun,
A squirrel slips upon a leaf,
While ants parade without a chief.

Bamboo sways with a bouncy beat,
Geckos groove with nimble feet,
Leaves chuckle as the rain does drip,
While flowers blurt, 'Let's take a trip!'

Giggling roots in playful strain,
Whispers of mischief in the rain,
Lush greens tease the wandering eye,
As butterflies flit, with a sly 'bye-bye.'

Caterpillars are dressed to impress,
In this wild, vibrant, green dress,
Join the laughter, the leafy cheer,
In this dance, we shed our fear!

When the Iguanas Sing

Iguanas strut with flair, oh my!
Beneath the trees, they catch the eye,
They croon their tunes, all day and night,
While insects dive and swirls take flight.

With every note, the petals sway,
And frogs start jamming just to play,
A symphony of greens and yellows,
Join the fun, forget your fellows!

Barking trees have jokes to tell,
As lizards laugh, 'It's going well!'
The sun winks at this quirky crew,
With every note, they sing it true.

So hear it now, the croaky cheer,
In this serenade, shed your fear,
For when the iguanas take the stage,
Life's a giggle, comes of age!

Mosaics of Rich Earth and Sky

In patches bright of green and blue,
Look closely now, find something new,
A patch of humor grows near the ground,
Where rainbow seeds scatter around.

Vines twist around like silly snakes,
Trying to outdo the fruitcakes,
As birds wear hats made of fine leaves,
And spin in circles, just like thieves.

The soil chuckles, a witty host,
Embracing bugs, it loves the most,
Layers of laughter sprinkled in,
As butterflies brag of their win.

So wander through this jestful land,
Where giggles sprout by nature's hand,
In every corner, tales unfold,
With mosaics bright, both brave and bold!

Where the Fireflies Whisper

Fireflies dance like sparkly fools,
In a rhythm that breaks all the rules.
Laughter bubbles in the cool night air,
As they flicker their lights without a care.

Buzzing bees wear tiny shades,
Sipping nectar in the sun's bright parade.
They concoct drinks so sweet and neat,
While flowers sway to their buzzing beat.

Silly frogs croak a tune so bold,
Telling tales that never get old.
The moon chortles, catching the fun,
As the garden glistens, kissed by the sun.

Come join the jest, oh what a sight,
In this place where laughter takes flight!
With nature's quirks, the glee won't cease,
In this whimsical, wild peace.

Blood-Red Blossoms and Silken Breezes

In the midst of petals, bright crimson hue,
Blooms gossip secrets like old friends do.
With whispers of pollen, they roll their eyes,
As butterflies plot their colorful lies.

A parrot squawks jokes, so crude and loud,
Making even shy petals burst from their shroud.
With each silly joke, the blossoms sway,
Hoping to stifle the giggles away.

The breeze pinches cheeks, feeling quite bold,
Leaving behind tales that never grow old.
And all the while, the sun shines bright,
Making mischief till the fall of night.

A dance of colors, a vibrant show,
Pinching the humbugs with a cheeky blow!
Come join this laughter, let spirits soar,
Among blood-red blooms, who could ask for more?

Moonlit Revelry in the Tropics

Under the moon's cheeky, silvery glare,
Creatures of the night begin to share.
A raucous cricket with tales of the past,
While a sleepy owl can't help but laugh fast.

Nightingales serenade with a wink,
While tree frogs ramble, causing a stink.
The wind carries giggles through the leaves,
As laughter spins like the webs of thieves.

Still, the stars chuckle, twinkling bright,
Peeking down on this whimsical sight.
They nudge each other, laughing with glee,
At the silly antics of bumblebee.

So let's dance together under this light,
In riotous fun until nearly bright.
In every chuckle and every smile,
We find joy in this moonlit while.

The Hidden Heartbeat of Wild Flora

In the brush where wild things shake,
Lies the heartbeat of the messy lake.
With giggles hidden among the trees,
And blushing blooms that dance with ease.

Cacti wearing shades, looking quite dapper,
Wave at the clouds, "Hello, what a caper!"
Their thorns sharp but their wit even sharper,
As they poke fun at the nearby harper.

Dandelion fluff takes flight and drifts,
As squirrels trade jokes, exchanging gifts.
They scamper around with a springy bounce,
Chasing after laughs that seem to flounce.

Listen closely, this flora sings,
With each chuckle, the wildness clings.
In vibrant whispers and jokes galore,
The heartbeat calls, let's laugh some more!

www.ingramcontent.com/pod-product-compliance
Lightning Source LLC
Chambersburg PA
CBHW072129070526
44585CB00016B/1585